BUSINESS ETHICS

IN RELATION TO THE PROFESSION OF THE

RELIGIOUS SOCIETY OF FRIENDS.

AN ADDRESS

BY

CHARLES RHOADS,

Of Haddonfield, N. J.

DELIVERED BEFORE THE FRIENDS' INSTITUTE FOR YOUNG
MEN, OF PHILADELPHIA,

Second Month 9th, 1882.

[Printed for distribution, especially among young men, already or about to be in business.]

In the interest of creating a more extensive selection of rare historical book reprints, we have chosen to reproduce this title even though it may possibly have occasional imperfections such as missing and blurred pages, missing text, poor pictures, markings, dark backgrounds and other reproduction issues beyond our control. Because this work is culturally important, we have made it available as a part of our commitment to protecting, preserving and promoting the world's literature. Thank you for your understanding.

BUSINESS ETHICS

IN RELATION TO THE PROFESSION

OF THE

RELIGIOUS SOCIETY OF FRIENDS.

Geo. Fox writes of himself, " when I came to eleven years of age, I knew pureness and righteousness. The Lord taught me to be faithful in all things, and to act faithfully two ways, viz.: inwardly to God, and outwardly to man; and to keep to yea and nay in all things."

These sentiments may be regarded as an index of the practical effects of the subsequent teachings of the early Friends respecting their dealings with men. They had their germ in that heart-work of the Spirit, which leads the true possessor of Christianity to be faithful in all things, as one answerable to his Maker for both thought and deed;; to observe the Divine rule of doing to others as we would that they should do to us. Wm. Penn says, in speaking of the reformers of that age, with whom he was associated in religious fellowship, that they pressed the *practical* part of religion. They were ostracised by the corrupt worldlings of Charles the 2nd's time for their singularity, and the sensual priesthood were so incensed at a sect who protested against tithes and a forced maintenance for ministers, that they bade their flocks avoid dealing with the adherents of Fox. Sewell informs us that such a ban did not long avail to destroy the trade of the persecuted Quakers, for the people soon discovered that their interest lay in employing men who were strictly honest and conscientious in all things. From the period of its rise, to the present day, the members of our Society, as a class, have had a reputation for conscientious dealing which it is worth while for us to investigate, and inquire by what method so valuable a feature of morality may be fostered and perpetuated. It is for this purpose that we have invited the young and active business men, who are now the representatives of Friends' principles, to meet and review some of the relations which the subject bears to our distinctive profession.

That "Honesty is the best *policy*," is a familiar and, perhaps, true adage; but in the outset, I wish to repudiate its soundness as a Christian rule of action. If our honesty springs from motives of *policy only*, it will fail in the hour of temptation, because it is based on selfishness,.

not on the deep principles of right and justice. The man that sells a good article to his customers, only because he hopes to secure their future trade, will find occasions when the prospect of gain will blow from another quarter, and his *policy* will shift with it. It is not *expediency*, nor the hope of temporal reward, but the love of God, and a reverent fear of breaking His commands, that are the foundation stones of true honesty, and the business ethics of the Christian.

This I believe to be the secret of the character for fair dealing won by the Society of Friends, in their origin and progress as a body of Christian professors. It was one of the fruits of that radical change from a state of nature to one of grace, which they insisted on from the outset. The aphorism that, "a corrupt tree cannot bring forth good fruit," emanating from the lip of Truth himself, brings us to the root of the matter. Man fallen, needs the new birth, a new heart.

This renewed nature will just as surely produce the fruits of righteousness as the old nature did evil things.

With this postulate established, it is still a pertinent inquiry how we are to apply the principles laid down to the every-day occasions of life, and what criterion the customs of society and trade may properly afford us in making such applications.

I know of no purer code of rules for our guidance in this inquiry than is contained in the advices and book of discipline issued by Philadelphia Yearly Meeting on trade and business. Every member of our Society should read and study these admirable counsels. Many a young man who has been sucked into the maelstrom of bankruptcy might have been saved from it by adopting their warnings. I will quote from them some paragraphs: "The standard which the world adopts, and even defends in its pursuit of trade, and its desire to gather riches, is not a safe one for the disciple of Christ. 'Men will praise thee when thou doest well for thyself;' and we sorrowfully see that this praise is often bestowed with but little regard to the means employed to acquire wealth. But we are taught by the Saviour, himself, that 'that which is highly esteemed among men is an abomination in the sight of God,' and we fear that it is true as respects some of the modes of conducting business and many of the schemes for procuring money which are resorted to in the present day. Earnestly do we desire that all our dear friends may be scrupulously on their guard, not to suffer their nice sense of Christian integrity to be blunted or benumbed by the examples which pass unreproved in the community, but steadily to adhere to that strict uprightness in all their transactions and converse, which becomes the disciple of Christ, and which so remarkably distinguished our worthy predecessors.

How exact were they in the fulfilment of their words and obligations! How careful to avoid all evasive and insincere dealings, and how conscientious not to engage in anything of a doubtful or objectionable character!"

BORROWING.

Borrowing capital to embark in business is often just and necessary, but it is liable to great abuse, and under some conditions is pernicious to both lender and borrower. Let us hear what Stephen Crisp, a noted minister and writer in the Society, says of it in a letter written by him in 1678 to a friend, viz: "I am sorry to have the present occasion of writing to thee, and would have forborne, if a necessity had not been upon me for the Truth's sake and for thine. I have a deep sense of thy danger, and that thou art in a way to dishonor thy testimony; for I am informed by several who love thee well, that they believe thou art run into about three hundred pounds debt, to set thyself up as a public shopkeeper. Alas! John, what is the rise and spring of this, and what will the issue be? Oh, consider, is this fitting thyself for thy testimony, and the keeping thyself from entanglements in thy warfare? Or is it not rather a making use of the name of the Lord and of Truth to plunder others by fair means or words to get a visible estate into thy hand? and then thou may be plundered of it by foul means. It is an easy matter to preach and incur fines when thou knowest others' goods must bear the loss; thou art on the surest side, and then if it be taken away at last, a whining complaint of suffering for Truth's sake must serve instead of paying thy debts, as it hath done too many already. Dear John, I wish thou would yet take my counsel and send every friend their goods home with the money thou hast sold of theirs; and take thee to thy employment where God blessed thee, and in which thou grew up."

This seems a severe reproof for what is so common in our day, yet it involves principles too much lost sight of and which apply to any time. Borrowing with the most honorable intentions of repayment by persons who have insufficient capital or estate of their own to make up possible losses, unless done with the most candid statement by the recipient of the facts, often amounts to a species of theft in its final consequences. From some observation I would advise no young man to borrow money to set up business until he had earned and saved by his daily labor twice the amount borrowed. Such a course would secure two valuable safeguards against future loss. He would acquire the habit of economy by saving from small sources and gain the business experience necessary to future success. We need a wholesome fear of incurring debt in the community to check the habits of extravagance in living, now so rife everywhere. Every man who buys on credit, even articles for personal consumption, before he has earned the means to pay for his purchase, is drawing on the future which he may never realize, and is to this extent unjust.

Let your personal and domestic expenses always be rigidly kept within the limits of your present income. Never anticipate that next month or year you will earn more. If such a hope should be realized, the surplus can be readily appropriated when in hand, if not, the coming time is only weighted with a double burden that must bring sorrow and probably sin.

TRUSTS.

I feel that I cannot emphasize too forcibly, the danger to all classes of tampering with money intrusted to their care by others. Defalcations and breaches of trust have grown frightfully common within the memory of many who are yet in the meridian of life. From the errand boy who collects small bills for his employer up to the confidential clerk and the bank and railway president, we read in the public press almost daily of instances of peculation. I have been robbed by five office boys who have been in my employ at different times within a period of twenty years, besides suffering from the unfaithfulness of collectors of mature years. I can enumerate eight members of my own profession (conveyancing) who have embezzled funds intrusted to their care for investment by others. Some of them, men advanced in life, engaged in large business and enjoying a wide reputation for integrity and skill in their profession. In other lines of business how numerous are the cases of unfaithfulness to trusts! Some who had the careful training of Christian parents, including members of our own Society, condemned to a felon's cell for this crime. Truly we may say, "let him that thinketh he standeth take heed lest he fall." Nothing is more likely to foster this temptation than a presumption of our own immunity from it. Self-conceit is an open door into which Satan finds an easy entrance. We must guard the *first steps* that would lead us to treat another's property as our own. Is it the duty of a lad to deposit his employer's money in bank? let him not tarry on the street to gratify his curiosity, lest it be stolen from him. The bank book should be returned without delay to the counting-house, in order that immediate proof may be given of his faithfulness. Does he collect a bill for goods sold, or pay a debt for the firm? the money should not lie in his pocket over-night if it can be possibly avoided. A memorandum of every cent received and paid should be kept by him and rendered up daily.

Executors, trustees, guardians, treasurers, brokers, and all persons acting in a fiduciary capacity, should scrupulously avoid borrowing the funds belonging to their trusts for their own accommodation, even for a short time, unless they give such security for it as a co-trustee may deem adequate. Such borrowing has been a fruitful source of loss and ruin to thousands, of latter time. It is an insidious temptation to many persons, who have the control of the funds of others, to draw upon them to meet an unexpected emergency in business, or indulge in a promising stock speculation, under the blinding plea that the means to replace the amount will be readily attained by expected receipts, or a profitable turn in prices. Such prospects are often illusory, and then, perhaps, the exigency of the case leads to further tampering with the trust property, in order to cover past deficiencies. Many a man who did not *set out* with the *intention* of acting dishonestly, has thus been led on, step by step, into deceit and crime.

As a rule, it is safest for all who have occasion to take charge of the property of others for considerable periods of time, to make special deposits in bank, or some substantial safe deposit company, in the name of such estate or institution, of all moneys pertaining to that particular trust as paid in, and drawing on them only for necessary payments to the same object. This obviates the mingling of one's private funds with those of others, thus offering an obstacle to unwittingly drawing on the latter for personal use, and it insures keeping a distinct account of the balance on hand to the credit of the person or corporation represented, in case of death. Furthermore, it affords the rightful parties the benefit of the accruing interest on the deposits, (where the institution pays any,) and it tends to keep the mind free from an insidious but false idea, that the property which we have in custody for others, is in any sense our own.

The following paragraphs taken from an editorial article in the *Public Ledger*, are appropriate to this branch of the subject:

"There is a general disposition to grade the guilt of injustice according to the degree of pecuniary injury which it inflicts; or the amount of gain which it secures.

"The robbing of a bank, the fraudulent transaction by which thousands of dollars are made to change hands, the heavy defalcation which involves whole families in ruin, meet with the public disgrace and reprobation which they deserve; but trifling invasions of right, small encroachments upon honor, unfaithful service, petty pilfering, broken promises, and a host of lesser breaches of good faith, pass by unnoticed, or receive only weak and inefficient censure. When no one is seriously hurt the common impression is that no great harm is done, and the margin which divides the right from the wrong is thus continually overstepped. Few persons pause to consider the effect of this toleration. Far from being merciful, it is cruel in encouraging and fostering the beginnings of a course that leads to shame and ruin. For injustice, dishonesty, and fraud do not spring into existence as full-grown crimes. They grow slowly, surely, and steadily from small beginnings. If we would war against them successfully, it is their germs that we should attack.

"Much of the injustice and corruption that now blots our mercantile and political honor has its source in this light and indifferent way, in which the beginnings of a dishonorable course are regarded. Even in the home and the school are such seeds sown and nurtured. Children are quick to perceive the standard of integrity held by those around them, and to catch the prevailing tone of feeling. So the young man just commencing life in the workshop, the store or the office, finds that up to a certain extent, slippery dealing is tacitly permitted—that if he avoid causing serious annoyance to his employers, and especially if he shrewdly advance their interest, he may practice, unnoticed, little secret appropriations, or use unfairly the time for which he is paid, and thus gradually he comes to use the limit of detection as his only standard of integrity.

"The manufacturer, in like manner, will adulterate his goods just enough to increase his profits, without lessening his sales; the tradesman will make undue charges when he expects no investigation; the employer will deal unfairly with those who have no redress.

"The whole principle of justice is thus utterly lost; for justice ever maintains an upright attitude; she disdains to consider the chances of detection or the hope of gain; she spurns the paltry enticements of secrecy, or the temptation to condone an offence because the gain is small. She is true in thought as well as in deed, in the least as much as in the greatest. It is this spirit alone that can purify our moral atmosphere and protect our community from the stains of dishonor."

The Life of Abraham Lincoln, by J. G. Holland, furnishes some pleasing illustrations of that straightforward honesty, which was so marked a feature in the character of this illustrious man.

When a young man, he was employed as clerk and manager of a store at New Salem, Illinois. Here, on one occasion, he sold a woman a little bill of goods, amounting in value by the reckoning, to two dollars and six and a quarter cents. He received the money, and the woman went away. On adding the items of the bill again, to make himself sure of correctness, he found that he had taken six and a quarter cents too much. It was night, and closing and locking the

the store, he started out on foot, a distance of two or three miles, for the house of his defrauded customer, and delivering over to her the sum whose possession had so much troubled him, went home satisfied.

On another occasion, just as he was closing the store for the night, a woman entered and asked for half a pound of tea. The tea was weighed out and paid for, and the store was left for the night. The next morning, Abraham entered to begin the duties of the day, when he discovered a four-ounce weight on the scales. He saw at once that he had made a mistake, and, shutting the store, he took a long walk before breakfast to deliver the remainder of the tea. His biographer remarks that these are very humble incidents, but they illustrate his sensitive honesty better perhaps than they would if they were of greater moment.

About this period of his life, he was appointed post-master for New Salem. The business and the emoluments of the office were both very small, and it was given to him, because he was the only man in the neighborhood willing to take it, who could make out the returns. Not willing to be tied to the office, as it yielded him no revenue that would reward him for the confinement, he made a post-office of his hat. Whenever he went out, the letters were placed in his hat. He kept the office till it was discontinued or removed, but his accounts with the post-office department were not settled till several years afterwards. In connection with this settlement, occurs an interesting exhibition of his rigid honesty.

It was after he had become a lawyer, and had been a legislator. He had passed through a period of great poverty, had acquired his education in the law in the midst of many perplexities, inconveniences and hardships, and had met with temptations, such as few men could resist, to make a temporary use of any money he might have in his hands. One day, seated in the law-office of his partner, the agent of the post-office department entered, and inquired if Abraham Lincoln was within. Lincoln responded to his name, and was informed that the agent had called to collect a balance due the department since the discontinuance of the New Salem office. A shade of perplexity passed over his face, which did not escape the notice of friends who were present. One of them said at once: " Lincoln, if you are in want of money, let us help you." He made no reply, but suddenly rose, and pulled out from a pile of books a little old trunk, and returning to the table, asked the agent how much the amount of his debt was. The sum was named, and then he opened the trunk, pulled out a little package of coin wrapped in a cotton rag, and counted out the exact sum, amounting to something more than seventeen dollars. After the agent had left the room, he remarked quietly that he *never used any man's money but his own.* Although this sum had been in his hands during all these years, he had never regarded it as available, even for any temporary purpose of his own.

MONOPOLIES.

Modern greed of wealth, and of its *rapid* acquisition, has led the ingenuity of men to devise and pursue schemes for its control unknown to any former age.

Combinations of capitalists are formed to create a "corner," not only in stocks, but in articles of daily and necessary consumption. What does this "cornering" imply? Why, that men already rich will buy up and hold in their grasp so large a proportion of the wheat, the sugar, the pork, the oil, or the cotton, in the market, that they can dictate the prices at which it shall be sold, and force buyers to pay more than it is intrinsically worth! Can this be reconciled with the precepts of the Sermon on the Mount, or loving one's neighbors as ourselves?

Again, we find merchants, already enjoying a good business, extending its dimensions from year to year, gradually absorbing the smaller stores around them, and by selling at very small profits, crushing out the prosperity of a large number of merchants of less capital in their vicinity. This may seem, according to the usual laws of trade, to involve no wrong. We may argue that it is a public benefit to have the goods we consume offered to us at the lowest possible price, and that great aggregations of capital, in a few emporiums, are essential to this result. But there are other considerations which enter into the estimate of such a policy, not to be overlooked. If a class of shopkeepers, who have heretofore made a moderate but comfortable independence for themselves and their families, are forced to relinquish their proprietorship in the trade, and accept subordinate positions in the employ of the great monopolists, they are at once made dependent for their daily bread on the continued success of the latter, and cannot rise above the scale of wages that they may earn in the effort to lay up a competence for old age. It degrades the many to the scale of subordinates, whilst it engorges the few with an excess of wealth, ruinous to them and their families. The case is similar in many lines of manufacturing. Formerly, the owner of a petty cotton or woolen mill on some rural stream, could, by patient industry and thrift, amass a comfortable little estate by the time he was sixty years of age. Now, the unpretending mill-wheel and loom are hushed and motionless, owing to the powerful combinations of stock-capital, which set on foot vast factories impelled by steam, and employing thousands of hands at low wages, and thus underselling the rustic manufacturer. If we really adopt the principles laid down by the Redeemer of mankind for our guidance in daily life, we cannot ignore such precepts as these, which we find recorded in the New Testament: "Lay not up for yourselves treasures upon earth, for where your treasure is, there will your hearts be also." "Ye cannot serve God and Mammon." "Verily, I say unto you, that a rich man shall *hardly* enter into the kingdom of Heaven." "Take heed and beware of covetousness, for a man's life consisteth not in the abundance of the things that he possesseth." "Do good and lend, hoping for nothing again. Give, and it shall be given unto you; good measure, pressed down and shaken together, and running over, shall men give into your bosom. For with the same measure that ye mete withal, shall it be measured unto you again."

Can these injunctions of the Divine Lawgiver be made to fit the measure of those monopolists in trade and manufactures who are striving to overshadow all others in the same line, and care not who goes down in the race, so they win?

EMPLOYERS AND EMPLOYEES.

It seems to me that those who control great capital and carry on a prosperous business are too forgetful, at times, of the Christian duty not to confine the salaries they pay to employees to the very lowest scale at which they can possibly procure them. I am aware that in seasons of financial depression, many extensive concerns are carried on at a cost which leaves little or no profit, and that economy in salaries and wages is essential to success at all times. But when prosperity does attend and large fortunes are being amassed by proprietors, surely they should open their hands wide to their poor brethren, whose labor is creating this wealth, and let them share in the bounty which comes from a common Lord and Father. Many boys and young men who are the sons of needy parents, enter counting-houses and manufactories at salaries too low to afford them even the cheapest kind of food and clothing. Their wages are so rated because it requires some time and experience to make their services fully valuable, and this is just. But the proprietor who has consecrated his silver and gold to a loving Saviour will not be slack to keep an eye to this class, and bestow charity in one of its best forms, by sending, perhaps at times, to the widowed mothers of such tyros who may be in his establishment, a bounty over and above the the weekly wages which the letter of his agreement demands.—"Because ye have done it unto one of the least of these, my brethren, ye have done it unto me." "Masters give unto your servants that which is just and equal; knowing that ye also have a Master in Heaven."

The obligations of those who are in the service of others are no less imperative than such as we have been enumerating. The Apostle exhorts both to a vigilant regard to duty. To the employed, he says, "be obedient to your masters, in singleness of your heart as unto Christ; not with eye-service as men-pleasers, but as the servants of Christ, doing the will of God from the heart. With good-will, doing service, as to the Lord, and not to men."

What an exalted standard of action is here proposed! and how does it elevate the lowest station in life to dignity when the incumbent fills it on such principles! In singleness of heart as unto Christ, not with eye-service! The clerk actuated by such motives requires no watching to stimulate to duty. His employer's interest is regarded as his own. No grudging stint of care and pains to perform his work in the best style, although out of sight and observation. The quick witness of a tender and enlightened conscience, keeping an even balance on the scale of labor and reward. Such a man is a cheerful workman: doing service with " good-will." No envy of the more-favored condition in life of those above him, but esteeming such as brethren in the Lord, whom to serve faithfully insures a higher reward than man can give.

SALESMEN.

Salesmen are often subjected to strong temptation to swerve from strict uprightness, either by the desire to effect large sales for their own profit on the commissions, or to gain favor with their employers. The tricks of trade used among unscrupulous merchants, easily blunt that fine sense of honor which should ever be present in the Christian mind, unless a watchful eye be kept to the unerring guide. John Field, in an address before the Young Men's Christian Association, on the subject of salesmen, said: "A salesman in my house, reported to me that he had succeeded in selling a very sharp merchant, a large bill. I was a little surprised myself, as I knew the merchant to be a very peculiar man. I found on looking into the matter, that all staple, well-known goods, were sold absolutely *below* cost, and other goods of which the buyer was not a critical judge, were charged *above* their market value. Calling the salesman into the office, I said to him: 'Mr. ———, I have always looked upon you as an honest man, until to-day.' His face crimsoned, and he became very angry, saying, 'Sir, do you mean to say that I am a thief?' I replied, 'You sold Mr. ——— a bill of goods, thus and so.' 'Yes,' he replied. I answered, 'In the first place, you sold some of our goods *below* cost, thus *cheating us;* in the second place, you sold *him* other goods *above* their market value; you cheated *him;* in other words, in the *day-time* you let him have his own way, but in the *mid-*

night hour, in the darkness, you had your way.' 'Mr. Field,' said he, 'I never saw it in this light before; you are quite right; I will never do so again.' And he never did.'"

A man placed his son with a merchant as a salesman. The youth in dealing with a customer, discovered *after* he had sold him a piece of goods, that it had an imperfection in it. This he informed the buyer of, as he was bound, of course, in honesty to do. The venal employer overhearing him, reprimanded him afterwards for his simplicity, in thus losing a profitable bargain, and threatened to discharge him if he repeated the act. The father of the salesman, with noble independence, upon being informed of the transaction, immediately re-called his son home, telling his employer that he would prefer that his boy should never become a merchant, rather than gain success on *such* principles.

INSOLVENCY.

The commercial panics and rapid decline in the value of all manufactured articles, that have grown chronic in the United States within the past fifty years, have involved so large a part of our merchants and manufacturers in failure and bankruptcy, that the public appreciation of the evil of insolvency is in danger of falling to a standard far below the true Christian rule, and much short of that maintained by the Society of Friends within the first two centuries of its existence. A recent writer states, that Governor Briggs of Mass., and Secretary Calhoun a few years ago, gave it as their deliberate opinion after diligent inquiry, that out of every hundred young men who come from the country to seek their fortunes in the city, ninety-nine fail of success. To this may be added the opinions of some of the shrewdest and most experienced business men in New York and Philadelphia, that not more than one per cent. of the best class of merchants succeed without failing in New York, and not more than two per cent. of those in Philadelphia retire on an independence, "after having submitted to the usual ordeal of failure."

The question very naturally arises, is this necessary and inevitable, or may a conscientious man so conduct his business that he can with reasonable certainty always be punctual to his promises, and just in the payment of his debts? We may answer that *some* have succeeded in doing so through a long course of years, covering more than one severe commercial crisis. One cause of their immunity from failure has been their adhesion to that salutary rule of our Church, to keep to moderation in their trade or business, and to live within the bounds of their circumstances. It is mainly, I apprehend, because men spend more on their families and selves than their net earnings warrant, and launch out in ventures beyond their capital, that disaster comes. Many are wrecked by indulging in speculations quite foreign to their regular and legitimate business.

It is generally easy for an insolvent to compound with his creditors for a release from further obligation by paying from 30 to 50 cents on the dollar. They may suspect that the debtor is withholding a comfortable provision for himself out of his assets, but the expense and delay of legal investigation, the disappointments resulting often from forcing the debtor through an assignment and a bankrupt court, all combine to induce creditors to accept almost any proposition the failing debtor may offer. Hence the growing danger, I fear, of laxity in estimating the true Christian duty of one under such trying circumstances, and that Friends as a Society may fall into the popular current which is so far below the golden rule of the Sermon on the Mount. The advice of Philadelphia Yearly Meeting in such cases is pertinent and just, viz.: "If any of our members appear unable to satisfy their creditors, they should be advised to call them together without loss of time and submit the state of affairs to their inspection, when if the creditors apprehend a surrender of the debtor's effects to assignees for the benefit of the whole to be necessary, let him be earnestly entreated to consent. It is the judgment of this meeting, that if persons so failing in their circumstances should at any time afterwards be favored with full ability to pay off their deficiencies, justice will require it of them, notwithstanding a composition with, and legal discharge from their creditors may have been obtained."

There are not wanting instances among Friends of this city, who have failed in business in early life and have been discharged upon payment of a part of their debts, afterwards retrieving their circumstances and discharging all former obligations with accrued interest. It is to be hoped that such honorable examples may be imitated by the present generation under like circumstances.

On the other hand, the duty of creditors to deal liberally with those whom the pressure of circumstances beyond their reasonable control may have involved in losses and actual inability to discharge their legal obligations is equally strong. The illustration cited by our Saviour to this effect, in the case of the servant who owed his lord ten thousand talents, and was forgiven when he had nothing to pay merely because of his importunity, should never be lost sight of by fallible beings. "I forgave thee all that debt because thou desiredst me; shouldest not thou also have had compassion on thy fellow servant, even as I had pity on thee?"

Many young men fail in their business enterprises for want of taking the counsel of those who are older, and have had experience in the same trade. It is characteristic of young Americans to imagine themselves capable of everything that any one else has ever done before them. They think it proof of a craven spirit to distrust their own abilities, or to consult with old fogies, as they term the prudent and cautious.

During the late war, a dashing General in the Union army, on starting out for a campaign through Virginia, was asked by his brother officers, where he proposed to establish his headquarters, and how he would maintain his communications and lines of retreat with the rear. He scoffingly replied, that his headquarters would be in the saddle, and as for his communications with the rear, he needed none, as a victorious advance only was to be thought of.

This boastful captain and his army was soon in full retreat before the enemy, leaving thousands of dead and wounded soldiers on the field of Manassas to the tender mercies of the rebels. Not much less presumptuous are those who despise the slow but careful and sure progress from small beginnings to final success, which have characterized the solid business men of Philadelphia.

Our natural self-esteem often leads us to overestimate our own ability for conducting large enterprises. Many a man would have been saved from disaster by advising with his father, or some experienced friend, before embarking in a commercial or manufacturing business that he was not qualified for. We want more of this disposition on the part of the young, to avail themselves of the experience of those who have passed through the rocks and shoals of commerce before them. Old men generally enjoy giving advice to the young, when it is sought in a confiding way, and it binds and strengthens those reciprocal feelings of sympathy and friendship that are so important in both civil and religious society, when this spirit of mutual confidence is cherished.

CONTRACTS.

To adhere strictly to the letter of a contract with another, when changes in the market after its being signed will entail a loss on the contractor, is recognized as high-toned integrity; but there should be felt also, on the part of him who reaps the benefit of such a bargain, a reciprocal duty to inquire how far it is honorable to permit another to lose under these circumstances. The following incident affords an example worthy of imitation: A merchant of New York, during the late war, made a contract with a mechanic to supply him with a quantity of tin cans. Not long after this, the price of tin rose so much that the contractor must lose money by completing the work at the price agreed upon. However, he said nothing, but went on delivering the cans. When the first bill for a part of them was received, the employer called upon him and said: "I understand you are losing money on this job." "Yes," replied the contractor, "but I can stand it; a contract is a contract, you know." "How much will you lose," asked the gentleman. "Oh, no matter," was the reply; "I don't complain, and you ought not to." "I insist on knowing." "Well, since you desire it, I shall lose so much a hundred," naming the amount. "Well, sir," said the noble-hearted man, "you must not lose this; it would not be right. I shall add the amount to your bill, and as the price of material may still rise, I will advance you the money for the whole of the contract, which, no doubt, you can now use to advantage." The difference thus paid, to which the contractor laid no claim, amounted to five hundred dollars. That was something more than business *honesty*. It was *Christian* principle carried out in business. The world needs just such examples to convince it of the truth of the Christian religion.

The following anecdote illustrative of faithful adherence to a contract which was not binding in law, but only in honor, and which required the sacrifice of $30,000 by one of the parties to it, is taken from a Boston newspaper:

"The late Samuel Brown, a merchant of Boston, and the owner of Brown's wharf, is still remembered by our older citizens. When the elder Quincy was Mayor, he saw the necessity of removing the Almshouse and the House of Correction to South Boston. Mr. Brown owned a very large vacant estate where the buildings now stand, and Mr. Quincy called upon him and stated his purpose to induce the City Government to remove the institutions to South Boston, and asked the price of the estate referred to. The reply was $30,000. Mr. Quincy said that would do, and asked thirty days' refusal and a bond for it, in order to endeavor to persuade the City Council to agree to the measure. Mr. Brown replied he should give no bond, as he said his word was his bond always. The Mayor took his word, and in twenty-eight days had obtained the proper authority, and again waited on Mr. Brown, saying that he had come to complete the sale of that land. 'What land?' said Mr. Brown. 'Why, the South Boston land we spoke of,' the Mayor said. 'At what price, sir?' asked the former. 'Thirty thousand dollars,' replied the latter, 'the price agreed upon.' 'Did I say that amount sir?' 'You did.' 'Have you any writing to that effect?' 'No sir, none.' 'Well,' said Mr. Brown, 'since you were here I have been offered $60,000 cash for it, and can you expect me to sell it for $30,000 to the city?' 'I do,' replied Mr. Quincy, 'because you agreed to.' 'Have you any proof of that?'

'Yes, I am witness.' 'But you, being an interested party, can't be a witness. Have you any other witness or proof, and do you ask me to refuse $60,000 for the land and sell it to the city for $30,000?' 'I do.' 'You have no bond for it, have you, Mr. Quincy?' 'None, sir, whatever,' replied the Mayor, stretching himself up with great dignity—'none whatever, but your word, and that you said was your bond.' 'And,' replied Mr. Brown, stretching himself up with equal dignity, 'so it is. My word is my bond, and for $30,000 the land is yours.'"

The sum of my argument, then is, this: That we stand in need of a religion that will wear in the counting-house, the market and the workshop, as well as in the sanctuary and home circle. That will stand as a barrier to injustice and fraud both in the small and great affairs of life. That will not permit its possessor to reserve the fairest and largest fruit for the top of the barrel, or mingle mahogany saw-dust with the cayenne pepper. That will keep the barytes out of pure white lead, and sand out of iron castings. That will bring all the unknown receipts of cash safely through the hands of the treasurer or agent into the coffers of his principal, just as surely as those which are known and expected. That will quicken the industry of the employee when no human eye could detect idleness; will bind the rich and the successful to look upon the prosperity of the needy and less favored as their peculiar care, before the increase of their own wealth—in a word that will, through the powerful chords of Divine charity, lead every man and woman to love their neighbors *as themselves.*

Such a religion we find inculcated in the pages of the New Testament, and exemplified in the life and person of its Divine Author. He is the Way, the Truth, and the Life. If we follow Him, we have His word of promise that we shall not walk in darkness, but shall have the Light of life. Nothing less than that transformation through faith in Him, and submission to the work of His Holy Spirit in the Soul, which He calls the *new birth,* can enable men to lay aside self-love, so far as to practice these exalted precepts. But this heart-cleansing grace, this infusion of God-like power *will* qualify finite man to do to others as he would that they should do to him. The history of the early Christians proves it, the annals of our own Society are rich in bright examples of such men and women, from its origin to the present day. It is to this spiritual force, *not of men,* but operating *in* all, if obeyed, that I desire to commend the young men for ability, for motive, for grace to resist all temptation to evil, and to pursue whatsoever is honest, just, true, and of good report in their commerce and labor among men. These are Ethical principles that must spread and pervade all classes of society, just in proportion to the increase of His government and kingdom, who came to save people from their sins. The unerring finger of inspired prophecy points to the day when the God of heaven shall set up a kingdom which shall never be destroyed through the instrumentality of the Stone cut out of the mountain without hands; and this power was destined to break in pieces and consume all other kingdoms. This King of kings was declared by the Prophet Daniel to be like unto the "Son of Man." He was to "make an end of sin, and to bring in everlasting righteousness."

The Redeemer of men when confronted with Pilate, and asked if he was a king, replied in the affirmative, and added, "To this end was I born, and for this cause came I into the world, that I should bear witness to the truth. Every one that is of the truth heareth my voice." His beloved disciple wrote of Him, "for this purpose was the Son of God manifested, that He might destroy the works of the devil. Whosoever is born of God, doth not commit sin. In this the children of God are manifest and the children of the devil. Whosoever doeth not righteousness is not of God." Now, I believe that it is for want of practical faith in these great truths, and because many teachers of Christian doctrine consider a life free from sin as utopian and impossible, that the standard of righteousness is so low, even among professing Christians. "This is the victory that overcometh the world, even our faith," is the language of an inspired Apostle. Fellow-soldiers in the combat against the world, the flesh and Satan, however we may have faltered in our ranks hitherto, and have yielded to temptation when sore pressed by the enemy of all righteousness, let us humble ourselves in the Divine sight, and confessing and repenting of those errors, look in faith for that forgiveness and cleansing from all sin, which is realized through the blood of Christ by those that walk in the light. Under His leadership let us press toward that mark for the prize of our high calling inscribed by our great Captain on his banner, "Be ye holy, for I am holy." Let us take to ourselves the whole armor of God, that we may be able to stand in the evil day, and having done all, to stand." To such, the kingdom of the Redeemer has already come, and the government of their conduct is upon His shoulder. They may accept and exult in the glorious promise that "He that overcometh, the same shall be clothed in white raiment; and I will not blot his name out of the book of life, but I will confess his name before my Father, and before His angels."

Printed by Libri Plureos GmbH in Hamburg, Germany